STEM CAREERS
ENVIRONMENTAL ENGINEER

by R.J. Bailey

Ideas for Parents and Teachers

Pogo Books let children practice reading informational text while introducing them to nonfiction features such as headings, labels, sidebars, maps, and diagrams, as well as a table of contents, glossary, and index.

Carefully leveled text with a strong photo match offers early fluent readers the support they need to succeed.

Before Reading

- "Walk" through the book and point out the various nonfiction features. Ask the student what purpose each feature serves.
- Look at the glossary together. Read and discuss the words.

Read the Book

- Have the child read the book independently.
- Invite him or her to list questions that arise from reading.

After Reading

- Discuss the child's questions. Talk about how he or she might find answers to those questions.
- Prompt the child to think more. Ask: Do you know anyone who works as an environmental engineer? What projects has he or she been involved in? Do you have any interest in this kind of work?

Pogo Books are published by Jump!
5357 Penn Avenue South
Minneapolis, MN 55419
www.jumplibrary.com

Library of Congress Cataloging-in-Publication Data

Names: Bailey, R.J., author.
Title: Environmental engineer / by R.J. Bailey.
Description: Minneapolis, MN: Jump, Inc., 2019.
Series: STEM careers | Includes index.
Audience: Age 7-10.
Identifiers: LCCN 2018020038 (print)
LCCN 2018021170 (ebook)
ISBN 9781641281836 (ebook)
ISBN 9781641281829 (hardcover: alk. paper)
Subjects: LCSH: Environmental engineers–
Juvenile literature. | Environmental engineering–
Juvenile literature.
Classification: LCC TA170 (ebook)
LCC TA170 .B35 2019 (print) | DDC 628.023–dc23
LC record available at https://lccn.loc.gov/2018020038

Editors: Jenna Trnka and Susanne Bushman
Designer: Michelle Sonnek

Photo Credits: ssuaphotos/Shutterstock, cover (wind turbines); stockphoto mania/Shutterstock, cover (hard hat); szefei/Shutterstock, 1; Patrick Foto/Shutterstock, 3 (girl); Tupungato/Shutterstock, 3 (drawing); Kokhanchikov/Shutterstock, 4; Manu Padilla/Shutterstock, 5; Gulf Images RM/Hashim/Diomedia, 6-7; llucky78/Shutterstock, 8-9; Nikifor Todorov/Shutterstock, 10; pedrosala/Shutterstock, 11; Dr Morley Read/Shutterstock, 12-13; Stephen Coburn/Shutterstock, 14-15; chinaface/iStock, 16-17; Ljupco Smokovski/Shutterstock, 18; nmedia/Shutterstock, 19 (girl); Gary Saxe/Shutterstock, 19 (dam); Steve Debenport/iStock, 20-21; domnitsky/Shutterstock, 23 (plant); urfin/Shutterstock, 23 (beaker).

Printed in the United States of America at Corporate Graphics in North Mankato, Minnesota.

TABLE OF CONTENTS

CHAPTER 1

EARTH'S KEEPERS

We only get one Earth. We must take care of it. Some people do this every day. Who?

Environmental engineers! They are keepers of the **environment**. They use science and **engineering** to care for Earth. How?

They look for ways to make fresh water. One way is **desalination**. This process removes salt from seawater. We need fresh water to live. But it is a limited **resource**.

DID YOU KNOW?

In the mid-1800s, London's River Thames was full of human waste. It made people sick. Joseph Bazalgette was a **civil engineer**. He led the construction of the city's first sewer system in 1858. It helped clean the river. People became well again.

desalination
plant

We reuse water. It gets dirty when we use it. Waste **pollutes** our water supply.

This means we have to clean it. How? Wastewater treatment plants. An environmental engineer helped design them! They also help find ways to use the waste removed from water.

TAKE A LOOK!

A wastewater treatment plant cleans used, dirty water. See how it works!

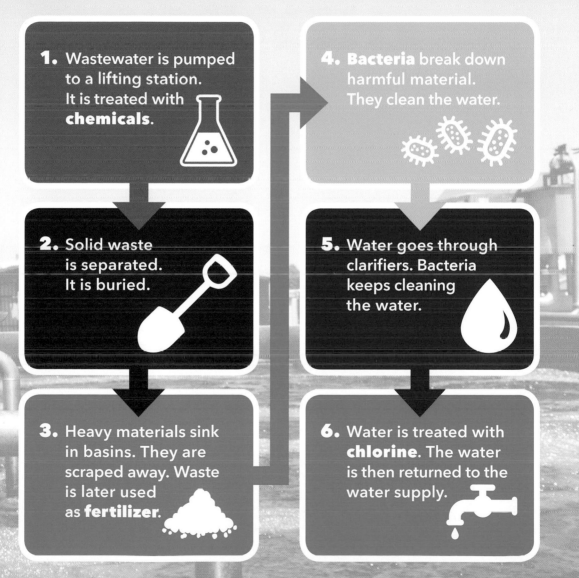

1. Wastewater is pumped to a lifting station. It is treated with **chemicals**.

2. Solid waste is separated. It is buried.

3. Heavy materials sink in basins. They are scraped away. Waste is later used as **fertilizer**.

4. **Bacteria** break down harmful material. They clean the water.

5. Water goes through clarifiers. Bacteria keeps cleaning the water.

6. Water is treated with **chlorine**. The water is then returned to the water supply.

CHAPTER 2

WHAT DO THEY DO?

Environmental engineers want to keep Earth clean. Cleaner **energy** is one way. Solar panels are an example.

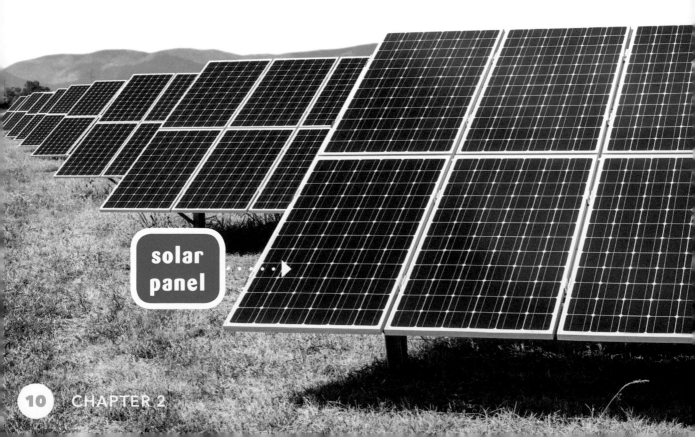

solar panel

So are wind turbines. Both produce energy. And reduce air pollution.

wind turbine

crops

They also study ways to feed more people. **Agroforestry** helps **crops** grow. How? Farmers plant trees among their crops. The trees help block crops from wind. They keep soil healthy, too. This produces more food!

They work with many people. Like who? Other engineers. Businesspeople. Builders. Why?

Let's say a builder is building a hotel. But what if it will harm the land? Environmental engineers may suggest a new spot. What else? Eco-friendly tools the builder can use. Like what? Solar panels.

builder

Many work in labs. Others work at building sites. Or at plants. They use instruments to gather air, water, and soil samples. What could they find in water? Lead. This would tell them the water must be treated.

Some work in offices. They use computers to write reports. Reports could explain ways to build structures that are better for the environment.

DID YOU KNOW?

They often wear gloves, masks, and safety glasses. This clothing protects them. From what? Harmful chemicals and waste.

CHAPTER 3

BECOME ONE!

As an environmental engineer, you could make a difference. How? You could find new ways to safely produce more crops. This will feed more people!

Is there a growing city near you? You could plan a new water supply system for it. You could help plan roads and dams that are safe for the environment.

In school, study **biology**. **Chemistry**. Math. Plan to spend four years in college.

Having a curious mind is important for this career. What would you want to work on? Maybe you could invent a new way to keep Earth clean!

DID YOU KNOW?

To work as an environmental engineer, you need STEM skills. What does STEM stand for? Science. Technology. Engineering. Math. STEM careers are in demand. They pay well, too.

ACTIVITIES & TOOLS

TURN SALT WATER INTO FRESH WATER

Environmental engineers work on ways to turn salty seawater into fresh water. In this activity, you will see that it is possible to change salt water into fresh water!

What You Need:
- 3 cups fresh water
- 1.5 tablespoons salt
- plastic wrap
- cup or small bowl
- large mixing bowl
- small rock

1 Pour 3 cups of fresh water into the mixing bowl.

2 Add the salt. Stir until it is dissolved.

3 Put the cup or small bowl into the mixing bowl. Do not let salt water get into the cup. If that happens, start over.

4 Place the plastic wrap over the bowl. Seal the edges.

5 Place the small rock on top and in the middle of the plastic. The plastic should bend slightly toward the cup.

6 Place the mixing bowl in a hot sunny area for one hour.

7 Drops of water should form below the plastic. The water should flow into the middle of the bowl. It should fall into the cup.

8 After a few hours, remove the plastic. The cup should now have water in it.

9 Taste the water in the cup. There should not be any salt! The sun evaporated the water in the mixing bowl. The water returned to its liquid state, but the salt stayed behind. You have removed the salt from the salt water!

GLOSSARY

agroforestry: A system in which trees or shrubs are grown among or around crops to improve the land's ability to produce the crop.

bacteria: Single-celled life forms that live in soil, water, plants, and animals and that sometimes cause disease.

biology: The study of life.

chemicals: Substances that cannot be broken down without changing into something else.

chemistry: A science that deals with the structure of substances and the changes they go through.

chlorine: A chemical that is used to clean water.

civil engineer: Someone who plans, designs, and builds transportation and infrastructure projects.

crops: Plants grown for food or feed for animals.

desalination: The process of removing salt from seawater; this is done in desalination plants that pull seawater from oceans and treat it.

energy: The ability to do work.

engineering: Using math and science to solve society's problems and create things that humans use.

environment: The surroundings or conditions in which a person, animal, or plant lives.

fertilizer: A substance that makes plants grow better.

pollutes: Makes the air, water, or soil unsafe to use.

resource: A supply of something.

TO LEARN MORE

Finding more information is as easy as 1, 2, 3.

① **Go to www.factsurfer.com**

② **Enter "environmentalengineer" into the search box.**

③ **Click the "Surf" button to see a list of websites.**

FACT SURFER